THEMATIC UNIT
APPLES

Written by Mary Ellen Sterling

Illustrated by Paula Spence and Keith Vasconcelles

Teacher Created Materials, Inc.
P.O. Box 1040
Huntington Beach, CA 92647
©1990 Teacher Created Materials, Inc.
Made in U.S.A.

ISBN 1-55734-266-0

Table of Contents

INTRODUCTION

Apples contains a captivating whole language, thematic unit. Its 80 exciting pages are filled with a wide variety of lesson ideas and reproducible pages designed for use with primary children. At its core are two high-quality children's literature selections, *Johnny Appleseed* and *The Giving Tree*. For these books activities are included which set the stage for reading, encourage the enjoyment of the book, and extend the concepts gained. In addition, the theme is connected to the curriculum with activities in language arts (including daily writing suggestions), math, science, social studies, art, music, and life skills (cooking, physical education, career awareness, etc.) Many of these activities encourage cooperative learning. Suggestions and patterns for bulletin boards and unit management tools are additional time savers for the busy teacher. Futhermore, directions for student-created Big Books and a culminating activity, which allow students to synthesize their knowledge in order to produce products that can be shared beyond the classroom, highlight this very complete teacher resource.

This thematic unit includes:

- ☐ **literature selections** — summaries of two children's books with related lessons (complete with reproducible pages) that cross the curriculum

- ☐ **poetry** — suggested selections and lessons enabling students to write and publish their own works

- ☐ **planning guides** — suggestions for sequencing lessons each day of the unit

- ☐ **writing ideas** — daily suggestions as well as writing activities across the curriculum, including Big Books

- ☐ **bulletin board ideas** — suggestions and plans for student-created and/or interactive bulletin boards

- ☐ **homework suggestions** — extending the unit to the child's home

- ☐ **curriculum connections** — in language arts, math, science, social studies, art, music, and life skills such as cooking, physical education, and career awareness

- ☐ **group projects** — to foster cooperative learning

- ☐ **a culminating activity** — which requires students to synthesize their learning to produce a product or engage in an activity that can be shared with others

- ☐ **a bibliography** — suggesting additional literature and non-fiction books on the theme

---

To keep this valuable resource intact so that it can be used year after year, you may wish to punch holes in the pages and store them in a three-ring binder.

Introduction (cont.)

Why Whole Language?

A whole language approach involves children in using all modes of communication: reading, writing, listening, observing, illustrating, experiencing and doing. Communication skills are interconnected and integrated into lessons that emphasize the whole of language rather than isolating its parts. The lessons revolve around selected literature. Reading is not taught as a separate subject from writing and spelling, for example. A child reads, writes (spelling appropriately for his/her level), speaks, listens, etc. in response to a literature experience introduced by the teacher. In this way, language skills grow naturally, stimulated by involvement and interest in the topic at hand.

Why Thematic Planning?

One very useful tool for implementing an integrated whole language program is thematic planning. By choosing a theme with correlating literature selections for a unit of study, a teacher can plan activities throughout the day that lead to a cohesive, in-depth study of the topic. Students will be practicing and applying their skills in meaningful contexts. Consequently, they tend to learn and retain more. Both teachers and students will be freed from a day that is broken into unrelated segments of isolated drill and practice.

Why Cooperative Learning?

Besides academic skills and content, students need to learn social skills. No longer can this area of development be taken for granted. Students must learn to work cooperatively in groups in order to function well in modern society. Group activities should be a regular part of school life and teachers should consciously include social objectives as well as academic objectives in their planning. For example, a group working together to write a report may need to select a leader. The teacher should make clear to the students and monitor the qualities of good leader-follower group interaction just as he/she would state and monitor the academic goals of the project.

Why Big Books?

An excellent cooperative, whole language activity is the production of Big Books. Groups of students, or the whole class, can apply their language skills, content knowledge, and creativity to produce a Big Book that can become a part of the classroom library to be read and reread. These books make excellent culminating projects for sharing beyond the classroom with parents, librarians, other classes, etc. Big Books can be produced in many ways and this thematic unit book includes directions for at least one method you may choose.

Johnny Appleseed Goes a'Planting

By Patsy Jensen

Summary

As a young boy John Chapman loved to help take care of the apple orchard, picking apples and eating them. His love of apples served him throughout his life.

As a young man he discovered a way to help pioneers on their way to Ohio. He gave them apple seeds to take with them. But when he found they would not have time to tend the trees, he decided it would be better if he planted the trees himself. Thus began the adventures of Johnny Appleseed as he traveled throughout the land, befriending both people and animals.

He spent his whole life planting and tending apple trees. Even today, people will often think of Johnny Appleseed whenever they see an apple tree.

The outline below is a suggested plan for using the various activities that are presented in this unit. You may adapt these ideas to fit your own classroom situation.

Sample Plan

Day I

- Daily Writing Activities: Food Journal, Sharing Session (page 34)
- Estimating Contest (page 6)
- Follow-up Activities (page 10)
- Read *Johnny Appleseed Goes a'Planting* aloud to class
- Complete the follow-up worksheet: A Johnny Appleseed Time Line (page 13)
- Assign Homework: Tall Tales (page 6)

Day II

- Continue Daily Writing Activities
- Share Homework
- Complete the follow-up worksheet: Larger Than Life (page 12)
- Essential Comprehension Activity: Time Line, #4 (page 7)
- Complete Worksheet: Some Facts (page 14)
- Apple Prints (page 11)

Day III

- Continue Daily Writing Activities
- Extend Homework: Read more tall tales
- Make a Sense Matrix after sampling apple products.
- Cook Applesauce (page 64)
- Science Worksheet: Parts of an Apple Flower (page 51)

Day IV

- Continue Daily Writing Activities
- Art: An Apple a Day Mobile (page 18)
- Math: Reading a Graph, Cooking with Apples (page 47)
- Science: Seeds Worksheet (page 52)
- Creative Writing: Apple Poems (page 30)

Day V

- Culminating Activity: Wheel Book (page 15)

Overview of Activities

Setting the Stage

1. Prepare your classroom for an Apple Unit. Set up an Apple Time bulletin board (see pages 68 to 73). Create a special Learning Center. See page 8 for how-to's on making a Learning Center.

2. Display a variety of apples, apple products, and apple-theme books (see page 79) at the Learning Center. A basket or a colander makes an attractive container for these articles.

3. Make an Apple Sense Matrix. (see pages 41 and 42.)

4. Learn about the four food groups (page 49 provides some background information) in preparation for the daily writing activities (page 34).

5. Grow seeds. For some sample experiments see page 22. Have the students record the progress of their plants in a Plant Diary (page 9).

6. Conduct an estimating contest. Display one apple with a sign that reads, "How many seeds do I have?" Children can place their guesses in a jar next to the apple. Follow up with the activities from page 10 and an art project from page 11.

Introduce the book *Johnny Appleseed Goes a'Planting* by explaining that it is the story about a man who tried to make his world better by planting apple trees. Then read the story to the class.

Enjoying the Book

1. As you read each part of the story, establish whether the incidents could have happened in real life or if they were exaggerations. For example, it is true that Johnny Appleseed's real name is John Chapman, but it is just a legend that he slept in a log with a bear.

2. Homework Activity: Direct the students to write one thing that could happen to them on their way home from school that evening. Then write an exaggeration of that event. You may wish to introduce this assignment by reading *And To Think That I Saw It On Mulberry Street* by Dr. Seuss. Follow-up activity: Larger Than Life worksheet, page 12.

   • In small groups of three or four have the children share their facts and exaggerations. Have each group choose the person with the tallest tale. Then in whole group, the tallest tales are shared.

   • Read other tall tales such as Paul Bunyan, Pecos Bill, John Henry, (see Bibliography, page 79.)

Overview of Activities *(cont.)*

3. *Johnny Appleseed Goes a'Planting* is illustrated by Pat Hoggan. Reread the story with the children spending time with the illustrations. Many of the pictures can be used as story starters.

4. Essential Comprehension Activity: Create a time line with index cards. Suspend a clothesline or heavy yarn across a section of a wall or bulletin board. Write a different event on each index card that you use (for examples, see page 13). Display all the events on a chalkboard tray. Have students choose which event occurred first; call on a student to attach the card to the clothesline with a clothespin. Continue in the same manner until all events are in correct chronological order.

Allow students to experiment with the time line on their own. Supply more index cards so that they can write other events to go in between the ones already on the line. As a follow-up activity, students can copy one event per page and illustrate it. Sequence all the pages together between a construction paper cover to make a book.

5. Complete the Some Facts worksheet, page 14.

Extending the Book

1. Make a Big Book. Use the sentence strips from page 13 and follow the directions on page 15. Or, make a Wheel Book using the pattern of directions from pages 39 and 40.

2. Make the "From Seed to Apple" Flap Book (pages 16 and 17).

3. After reading *Johnny Appleseed Goes a'Planting*, read *The Story of Johnny Appleseed* by Aliki. Compare and contrast the two versions. Make a Venn diagram to show their likenesses and differences. Conduct a class poll to find out which version the students liked better. Make a bar graph of the results. This activity can also be done by comparing *Johnny Appleseed Goes a'Planting* to *Miss Rumphius* by Barbara Cooney.

4. Construct An Apple a Day mobile. See page 18 for patterns and directions.

5. Use the Apple Time Bulletin Board. Make one apple for each student. After they have read a book about apples (see Bibliography, page 79, for suggested titles), have them write the title, author, and a short review of the book on their apple. Attach to the bulletin board. Or, write an apple word problem on each apple. (See sample word problems, page 45). Place the problems in the basket on the bulletin board. Write answers to the problems on apples on the tree. Have students match the problems to the answers. For more ideas, see the Directions on page 68.

Creating a Learning Center

A Learning Center is a special area set aside in the classroom for the study of a specific topic. Typically, a Learning Center contains a variety of activities and materials that teach, reinforce, and enrich skills and concepts. Because students learn in different ways and at different rates, a Learning Center can be a valuable means of providing for these differences. Activities in a given center should be based on the abilities, needs, and interests of the students in your classroom. Learning Centers are equally appropriate for cooperative group and individual use.

How to Create a Learning Center

- Select a theme or topic in any subject area.
- Label the center attractively with a display or poster.
- Determine specific skills or concepts to be taught or reinforced, e.g. kinds of seeds, parts of a flower.
- Develop appropriate learning activities, e.g. A Is for Apple Gameboard (page 53-54), Sense Matrix (page 42).
- Prepare extended activities for reinforcement or enrichment, e.g. Wheel Books (page 15), Apple Prints (page 11).
- Gather all materials needed to complete the projects at this center, e.g. paint, construction paper, apples.

Scheduling Center Time

- Plan a rotating schedule where groups of children are rotated to different activities. For example, one group can be attending a teacher-directed lesson, while the second group completes seat work, and the third group is at the Learning Center.
- Assign individuals or small groups to the center according to diagnosed needs.
- Have a set Center Time each day. Assign a different group each day to work at the center during that time.

Record Keeping

- Supply each student with a Learning Center Record Keeper (page 75). They can easily keep track of the activities that they have completed.
- Make a monthly calendar for each student (see page 74); store in a three-ring binder at the Center. Record information on the appropriate spaces.
- Keep a file box with students' names listed alphabetically on index cards. Record notes and activities completed on the cards.

| Name: | Date: |

Plant Diary

Watch your plant grow. Write what you see. Then draw a picture.

Day _____ Date _____

What I saw: _____

_____

_____

A picture:

Day _____ Date _____

What I saw: _____

_____

_____

A picture:

Day _____ Date _____

What I saw: _____

_____

_____

A picture:

Day _____ Date _____

What I saw: _____

_____

_____

A picture:

Name:	Date:

I Wonder...?

1. Cut an apple in half around its middle. What pattern do you see? Draw a picture.

2. Get an apple. Guess how many seeds are in the apple. Write your guess in the box.

Now, cut your apple in half the long way. Count the seeds. Write the number in the box.

Did you make a good guess?_____

Apple Fractions

3. This apple has been cut into two equal pieces. Each piece is one half. Color one half.

Here is another way to write one half. Trace the fractions.

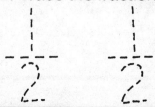

4. This apple has been cut into four equal pieces. Each piece is one fourth. Color one fourth.

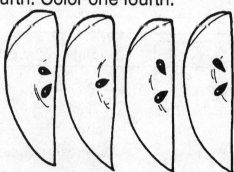

Here is another way to write one fourth. Trace the fractions.

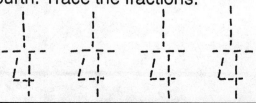

Apple Art

Apple Prints

Materials: foam meat trays or plates; undiluted liquid red, green, and yellow tempera paint; apples cut in halves; white construction paper.

Directions:

- Pour paint into trays or plates.
- Dip apple (flat surface down) into paint tray.
- Press onto construction paper.
- Repeat to make a pleasing design.

*Apple Prints can also be used to make a border for a bulletin board. Or, create a class mural. Draw a large tree outline on butcher paper; have students make apple prints on the tree.

Apple Collage

Materials: magazines; scissors; glue; tagboard or cardboard.

Directions:

- Cut out pictures of apples, apple recipes, and apple products from magazines.
- Arrange on the tagboard; glue pictures, etc. to the tagboard.
- Coat with shellac or, if the piece is flat, laminate.

Brainstorm apple words with the class (round, red, sweet, etc.). In small cooperative groups, students choose one word and collect pictures, recipes, food labels, words, etc. that depict that word. **Variation**: Direct students to make a collage of words and phrases that describe apples.

Watercolor Apples

Materials: Watercolors; paint brushes; construction paper; scissors; glue.

Directions:

- Paint shades of watercolors all over one sheet of construction paper.
- Let dry overnight.
- Cut or tear apple shapes from the watercolored paper.
- Glue the shapes to a sheet of construction paper (a contrasting color is especially effective).

*Draw a simple outline of a tree onto a large sheet of tagboard or butcher paper. Have students glue their apples to the tree background.

Name:	Date:

Larger Than Life

Sometimes people say things to make them greater than they are—they "stretch" the truth. For example, they say that Johnny Appleseed's feet were as tough as elephant's hide.

Read the sentences below. Color the apple next to each one that stretches the truth.

1. After a long hike in the woods, the boy was as hungry as a bear.

2. The cat was as quick as lightning as he chased the mouse.

3. Mud splashed all over her new dress as she crossed the street.

4. Our new swimming pool is as deep as the ocean.

5. This box is light enough for me to carry by myself.

6. Her doll house is as big as a castle.

Draw a picture of this stretched truth: *It's raining cats and dogs.*

12

Name:	Date:

A Johnny Appleseed Time Line

Work with a partner for this activity.

Cut apart the sentence strips. Glue each strip to a sheet of construction paper. Draw a picture for each sentence. Put the sentence/picture pages in story order and fasten one side to make a book.

Both animals and people were friends to Johnny.

Johnny gave pioneers apple seeds to plant.

As a boy he enjoyed taking care of the apple orchard.

Johnny saw the trees he planted bloom before he died.

Johnny Appleseed was born on September 26, 1774.

He set out to plant apple trees in Ohio.

Name:	Date:

Some Facts

Word List

tales

Chapman

autumn

orchards

bear

apples

Ohio

September

How much do you know about Johnny Appleseed? Fill in the blanks with words for the Word List. Then write the words in the Crossword Puzzle.

Across

2. Johnny planted _ _ p _ _ seeds.

5. He was born in the month of _ _ _ _ _ m _ _ _.

6. He planted seeds in _ _ _ o.

7. Johnny spent the night with a _ _ _ r in a log.

Down

1. People tell tall _ _ l _ _.

2. Apples are picked in _ u _ _ _ _.

3. Johnny's last name was _ h _ _ _ _ _.

4. Apples are grown in _ _ _ _ _ _ r _ _.

14

How to Make a Big Book

This is a simple variation of Big Books for students to make.

- Group the students in small, cooperative groups of two or four.

- Divide sentence strips (page 13) or index cards (page 7) among group members.

- Glue each sentence strip or card to a sheet of construction paper.

- Illustrate the text with drawings, finger painting, collages, etc.

- Cut an apple shape from red construction paper.

- Fold back the top of the apple and paste the flap to the right side of a large piece of colored tagboard.

- Staple the story pages (one on top of the other) to the left side of the colored tagboard.

- Lift the apple flap and underneath it write "Written and Illustrated by." IIave the students sign their names.

How to Make a Wheel Book

Wheel books add interest and excitement to a writing project, so they are well worth the extra effort. You may have to cut out the spaces on the apple shapes; some children might require help attaching the paper fastener to the circle.

- Divide the class into cooperative groups of two or three students.

- Make enough apple and circle patterns for each group (patterns are on pages 39 and 40).

- Enlarge the cut-out space, if desired.

  - Attach the circle behind the apple shape.

  - Have the students draw a picture in the space.

  - Rotate the circle until the picture is covered and draw another picture.

  - Continue in the same manner until the story of Johnny Appleseed has been told in pictures.

- Have two cooperative groups at a time share their books with one another; change groups until all stories have been shared with everyone.

- As a follow-up, direct students to write a sentence for each story picture. Or, instead of drawing pictures in each space of the circle, write a sentence.

Name:	Date:

"From Seed to Apple" Flap Book

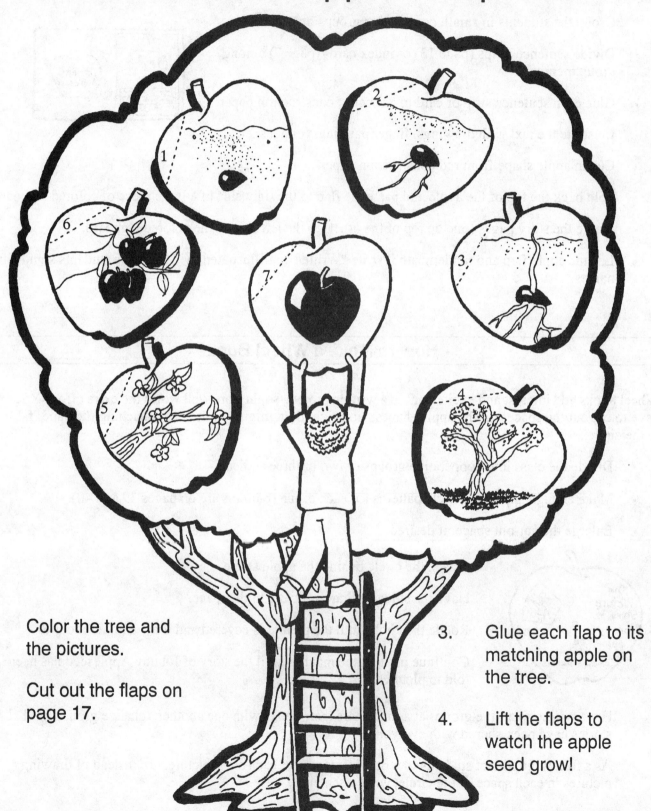

1. Color the tree and the pictures.

2. Cut out the flaps on page 17.

3. Glue each flap to its matching apple on the tree.

4. Lift the flaps to watch the apple seed grow!

16

Name:	Date:

"From Seed to Apple" Flap Book *(cont.)*

1. Color and cut out the apples.

2. Glue the flaps to the matching spaces on the tree.

3. Bend back at the dotted line.

1. A seed is planted.

Flaps

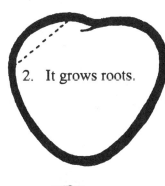
2. It grows roots.

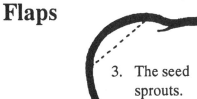
3. The seed sprouts.

4. It grows into a tree.

5. Flowers begin to blossom.

6. Apples are growing.

7. An apple at last! YUM!

Extensions:

- Sing and play "Round the Apple Tree" (page 61).

- Have cooperative groups of children write their own "seed-to-full-grown plant" story. Topics could include different kinds of seeds: beans, wheat, water lilies.

- Draw a germinating seed; label the seed skin, root, and seed leaves.

- Grow seeds between two pieces of moist blotting paper. Remove the top piece just long enough to observe daily growth. Keep paper moist. Have the students log the daily progress with words and pictures (see Plant Diary, page 9).

Day 1

Day 3

Day 5

An Apple a Day Mobile

diagram

An apple a day...

An apple a day . . .

Directions:

· For each mobile, make two sets
  of pattern pieces. (Duplicate patterns onto colored construction paper or use white paper and color
  the pattern pieces).

· Glue a 16"(40cm) length of yarn down the center of the pattern pieces (see diagram above).

· Glue the other set of patterns on top of the yarn and these pieces.

· Brainstorm some endings for the worm's expression on the top half of the apple.

· Have students write their own endings on the bottom half of the apple.

· Hang the mobile.

The Giving Tree

by Shel Silverstein

Summary

There once was a tree who loved a boy. The boy would visit daily and gather its leaves, climb its trunk, swing from its branches, and eat its apples. The boy loved the tree.

As the boy grew older, the tree was often left alone. When the boy came back because he needed money, the tree gave him apples to sell. Later the boy needed a house for his family, so the tree gave his branches to the boy. When the boy became an old man, he needed a quiet place to rest. He sat on the tree stump and the tree was happy once again.

Simple line drawings add to the delight of this tender tale. The concepts of giving, acceptance and love are described in a manner that children of all ages will be able to recognize and understand.

The outline below is a suggested plan for using the various activities that are presented in this unit. You should adapt these ideas to fit your own classroom situation.

Sample Plan

Day I

- Daily Writing Activities: A Week of Writing (page 35)
- Brainstorming (page 20)
- Plant Bean Seeds (page 22)
- Read *The Giving Tree* aloud to class
- Complete Worksheet: A Tree of Many Gifts (page 26)
- Assign Homework: Happiness Is... (page 24)

Day II

- Continue Daily Writing Activities
- Share Homework
- Check progress of bean seeds (page 22)
- Essential Comprehension Activity: Role Playing #5 (page 21)
- Language: Match the Words worksheet (page 27)
- Apple Word Collage (see Variation, page 11)

Day III

- Continue Daily Writing Activities
- Extend Homework: Make a class book (page 20)
- Science: Things From Trees worksheet (page 28)
- Make Apple Smiles (recipe page 64)
- Creative Writing: An Apple Chain Story (page 41)

Day IV

- Continue Daily Writing Activities
- Art: Watercolor Apples (page 11)
- Math: Feelings worksheet (page 23)
- Check progress of bean seeds
- Creative Writing: Apple Expressions (page 41)
- Science: Make a Tree. Use Chart (page 25)
- Culminating Activity: Bulletin Board Story (page 21)

Overview of Activities

SETTING THE STAGE

1. Set the mood in the room with an appropriate display at a Learning Center (see page 8 for how-to's on creating a Learning Center). Fill a large grocery bag or a cardboard box with foods and objects that come from trees. Fill a plastic sack with some things that do not come from trees.

2. Brainstorm with the whole class. Make two lists: things that come from trees; things that do not come from trees. Assign partners. Direct them to make a chart of Things From Trees and Things Not From Trees. Have them write the words and draw pictures.

3. Plant bean seeds. (They are hardy and they grow quickly!) Supply each child or cooperative group with an egg carton, soil, and eleven seeds. Direct the students to plant ten of the seeds and save one for comparison. See page 22 for complete procedures.

4. Discuss trees and how they help people with all the things they give us. Explain that *The Giving Tree* is one tree's story about how he helped a boy throughout his life.

ENJOYING THE BOOK

1. Read *The Giving Tree* aloud to the children. At each stage of the boy's life discuss some other ways the tree could have been useful to the boy. For example, the boy plays on a swing from the tree. How else could he have played on the tree (climbing; build a tree house, etc.)?

2. At each stage of the boy's life, discuss how the tree feels. Make lists of words. Compare the beginning list with the ending list. Complete the Feelings worksheet (page 23).

3. **Homework Activity:** Complete Happiness Is... worksheet (page 24).

4. **Extend the Homework Activity.** After the students have shared their responses to Happiness Is..., punch holes on the left side of each homework sheet. Place all activity sheets into a looseleaf binder. Allow students to decorate the cover. Keep the book at a Learning Center or special area so that students can read their book during free time.

Overview of Activities *(cont.)*

3. Display the tree chart (see page 25); you may wish to enlarge it using an overhead projector. Direct students to draw and label their own tree. Children may work in small groups to complete this activity.

4. **Essential Comprehension Activity**: Group students in cooperative groups of two or three. Give each group a copy of A Tree of Many Gifts worksheet (page 26). As a group, they must determine the order in which the events took place. Write each on the proper line. As a follow-up activity, students can copy each line on a separate page and illustrate the event. Put the pages in order. Hang them on the wall for everyone to read. Encourage students to add other events from the story to their writing.

5. Choose five students of varying heights. Direct them to arrange themselves in order from shortest to tallest. Have each student role play the boy at various stages of his life. The shortest person plays the boy at his youngest; the tallest person plays the boy at his oldest. Each character in turn tells what he wants from the tree and why. Students could also make signs and hold them up for the class to read.

6. Use the Match the Words worksheet (page 27).

EXTENDING THE BOOK

1. Make a bulletin board story. Group the children and have each group make a character in large form. The different ages of both the man and the tree should be represented. Attach the characters to a bulletin board background. Add a speech bubble to each character and have the students write something their character said in the story. The children can read the bulletin board as part of their shared reading time.

2. Trees provide us with many useful foods and materials. Research these with the children in a science lesson. Use the Things From Trees worksheet (see page 28). Students are to find seven things that come from trees.

Planting Procedures

Plant and do some simple experiments with bean seeds. They are very hardy plus they grow quickly so children can see results right away. Below is a list of necessary materials and directions for procedures. Students can do these experiments individually or they can work in cooperative groups.

Materials

One egg carton per student or group; soil; eleven bean seeds per student or group; scissors; marking pen; craft sticks; water.

Procedure

- Cut the lid off of the egg carton; place the bottom half onto the lid.
- Have the students label the egg cartons with their names.
- Fill ten egg cups with soil; put one bean in an empty cup.
- Poke a hole in the soil with a craft stick (a finger works just as well).
- Place a bean seed in the hole.
- Cover the seed with soil.
- Plant nine more seeds the same way.
- Sprinkle water on the soil.
- Put the egg carton in a place where it will get sun.
- Water the seeds a little each day.

Experiments

- Place some egg cartons in sunlight, some away from direct sunlight, and the remaining one in a dark space (such as a closet). Compare the growth. Which ones grow best?
- Place all egg cartons in sunlight. Divide them into three labeled groups. Group I is watered every day. Group II is watered every other day. Group III is not watered at all. Have students predict the results and compare with what actually happens.
- Place all egg cartons in sunlight; water daily. After three or four days dig up one seed. Has it changed? How? Students can describe and illustrate the changes in a Plant Diary (page 9). Every few days dig up another seed for observation. Continue until the plants push through the ground. Continue to record changes in appearance.
- **Extensions:** Have the students draw the stages in the germination of a bean seed (diagram below). Label the parts of a seed.

1.   2.   3.   4.   5.

22

Name:	Date:

Feelings

The tree and the boy had many feelings in the story *The Giving Tree*. To find out some of these feelings, answer the math problems. Then place the letter that's next to your answer in the correct blank. Some clues are given to help you.

3 +3 ____ R	8 +8 ____ D	5 +5 ____ H	12 +12 ____ Y	6 +6 ____ T

9 +9 ____ N	10 +10 ____ S	4 +4 ____ P	11 +11 ____ V	7 +7 ____ L

1. The tree __ o __ e __ the boy very much.
          14   22   16

2. The boy was __ a __ __ __ when he played in the tree.
               10   8 8 24

3. The boy grew older and the tree was often a __ o __ e .
                                                14   18

4. The tree felt __ a __ .
                 20   16

5. The boy grew old. He was very __ i __ e __ as he sat on the tree.
                                    12   6   16

6. The tree was __ a __ __ __ once again.
                10   8 8 24

Name:	Date:

Happiness Is...

When the boy was young, he was very happy with the tree. Draw four things that make you happy. Write a sentence about each one.

_____ _____	_____ _____
_____ _____	_____ _____

24

Tree Chart

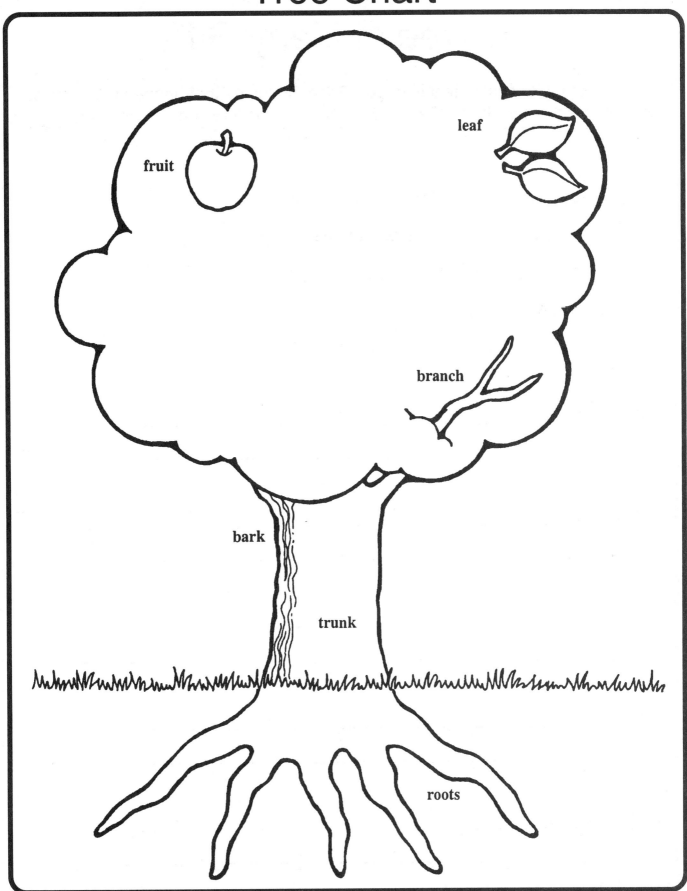

fruit

leaf

branch

bark

trunk

roots

Name:	Date:

A Tree of Many Gifts

Work as a group to complete this page. Read the things that happen in the story. Decide in which order they belong. Write them on the lines below. Draw pictures for each sentence.

- The boy cuts the tree trunk to make a boat.

- The boy sits down and rests on the tree stump.

- The boy plays "King of the Forest."

- The boy gathers apples to sell.

- The boy uses branches to build a house.

First: _____

_____

Second: _____

_____

Third: _____

_____

Fourth: _____

_____

Fifth: _____

_____

Name:	Date:

Match the Words

Cut out the word circles at the bottom of the page. Paste them next to the characters who said them.

"...I have nothing left to give you."

"I don't need very much now..."

"I want to buy things and have fun."

"Take my apples, boy, and sell them in the city."

"I want a boat that will take me far away from here."

Name:	Date:

Things From Trees

Many foods that we eat are grown on trees. Many things that we use are made from the wood. Find and color seven things in the picture below that come from trees. Trace the words in the Word List.

Word List

bag   lemons

oranges   money

pencil   pears

newspaper

28

Apple Chants

This mini-unit can be used any time during the Apples Unit. If preferred, single activities from this mini-unit can be incorporated into your apple studies.

Writing an Apple Chant

1. Duplicate the Apple Chant below on chart paper for all the students to see. Or write the chant on the chalkboard or an overhead projector. Have students copy the words.

2. Read the words together. Model the chant for the students. Then have the students chant together. Be sure to place the accent on the underlined words.

Apple Chant

I see apples all <u>around</u>.

Apples on the <u>tree</u>.

<u>Red, yellow, green.</u>

Apples on the <u>ground</u>.

<u>Blue, purple, brown.</u>

I see apples all <u>around</u>.

3. Brainstorm with the class. Discuss the different apples they have seen and tasted. Create a Word Bank on chart paper or an overhead projector.

Apple Word Bank		
Colors	**Looks**	**Places**
red	shiny	a store
yellow	bright	a basket
green	smooth	an orchard

4. Make a large chart of the worksheet on page 33. With the whole group, model filling in the blanks with words from the Apple Word Bank.

5. Group students in workable pairs. Have them create their own chants. They may use words from the Apple Word Bank or brainstorm other words.

More Poems

Sense-ative Poems

"Sense-ative" poems can be written by small cooperative groups of three or four. Provide one apple for each group and three index cards (or strips of construction paper) per student. First, direct the students to observe the apple. How would they describe it in one word? (red, shiny, smooth, etc.). Each student in each group writes one descriptive word on an index card. Next, have students take turns holding the apple. How does it feel? (smooth, firm, solid, etc.). Again, each student should write one descriptive word on an index card. Now cut the apple into thirds or fourths and direct the students to eat their apple slice. How does it taste? (sweet, juicy, tangy, etc.). Students are to write one descriptive word on their last index card. Direct the groups to arrange their index cards into a poem. Give them extra index cards so they can write other words. Have the groups share their poems. (Note: Students do not have to use all of the descriptive words.)

Example | Apples

Apples	are	red	round	and	sweet
	so	delicious	to	eat	
They	are	firm	solid	and	bright
	Just	an	absolute	delight	

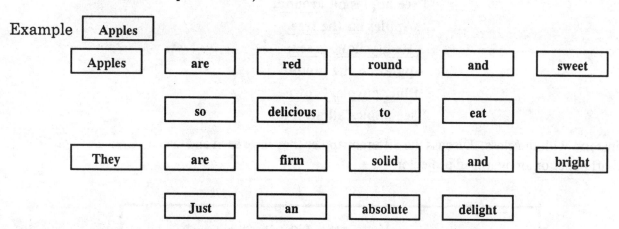

Display the poems on a wall or bulletin board.

Apple Couplets

Clever apple, fat and round. To think I found you on the ground!

Provide the first line of a couplet or two-line rhyming poem. Then brainstorm words that rhyme with the last word in the line. Together the class can create a second line. Pair the students and have them write and illustrate their own couplets.

Sample first lines:
- Six little apples sitting in a row...
- One lone apple in an apple tree...
- Apples on a moonlit night...

Art Activities

Art Activities

Make Funny Faces from apples (page 32). Use the expressions on the faces as a basis for some Funny Face poems. Or make Salty Pictures (page 32). Students can make apple pictures using this method and write a poem on the same page.

Class Books

After the students have written and illustrated their chants, poems, or couplets, make a construction paper cover and bind all the pages together with metal rings or staples. Add it to the classroom library. Share it with another class.

Cooking Activities

Apples are a versatile fruit; they can be prepared in main dishes, as desserts, and even as drinks! You will find some tasty treats to make on pages 64 and 65. Have students describe their treats in poetic form using the "sense-ative" poem method from page 30.

Can Rain Make Applesauce?

Read Rain Makes Applesauce by Julian Scheer. This unique book of silly talk is sure to inspire the most reluctant writer to create some unique nonsense poems.

Shapely Poems

Have pairs or small groups of students work together on this project. Direct them to draw an outline of an apple (or use a pattern such as the apple stationary on page 76) on construction paper or plain white paper. Next, have them brainstorm a list of all the words they can think of that are related to apples. Then they must write their words along the outline of the apple.

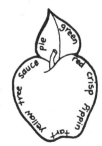

Art Activities

Funny Faces

Materials: apples; apple corer; plastic knives; pipe cleaners; lemon juice; bowl; water

Directions:

- Peel and core the apples.

- Use the plastic knife to make slits for the eyes and the mouth. Cut a wedge nose and shape a chin and cheeks.

- Fill a bowl half way with water. Add two tablespoons of lemon juice.

- Soak the apples in the lemon water for twenty minutes.

- Remove the apples. Thread a long pipe cleaner through the core and twist the ends together to make a hook.

- Hang the apples in a warm, dry place for four days. Watch as the faces slowly shrink and change.

Salty Pictures

Materials: salt; dry powdered tempera paints; drawing paper; paint brushes; plastic margarine cups; liquid white glue.

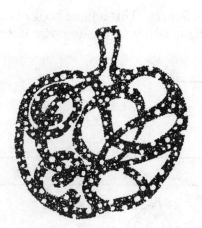

Directions:

- Mix some salt and dry tempera paint in a plastic margarine cup. (Use a separate cup for each color paint you mix.)

- Brush or dribble the liquid glue in an apple pattern on the drawing paper.

- Sprinkle the salt and paint mixture over the pattern.

- Use as many colors as desired.

- When the glue dries, gently tip the picture over a trash can to remove the excess colored salt.

- The salt crystals will make a sparkling apple picture.

32

Apple Chant

With a partner write an apple chant. Illustrate your chant in the box below.

Written and Illustrated by:

_____

_____

I see apples_____.

Apples on the _____.

_____,_____,_____.

Apples on the _____.

_____,_____,_____.

I see apples_____.

Daily Writing Activities

Food Journals

Each student will need a Journal Worksheet (see page 36) for each day's writing. Pages can be stapled together between a folded sheet of construction paper; students can decorate their journal covers, if they wish. This activity should be started as soon as they get to their seats in the morning.

Instruct the students to keep a food journal of what they ate for dinner the previous evening. They do this by listing the foods in the proper sections of the food group graph on their Journal Worksheet. Then have them answer the questions on the page. (A lesson on food groups will be necessary before beginning this activity. A good resource is TCM-212, *Food and Nutrition*. Also, see worksheet, page 49.)

Sharing Sessions

Divide the class into small groups of three to five. One at a time they share their menus and suggestions for making the meals more nutritious. The others in the group can then make more suggestions on ways to improve the meal.

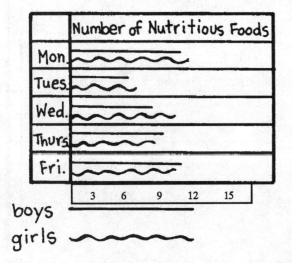

Graphing

As a whole group determine how many students ate a well-balanced dinner each night. Graph the results on the chalkboard or on chart paper each day; graph boys and girls separately (or use some other way to divide the class). At the end of the week analyze the results. How did the number of nutritious meals differ from the beginning of the week to the end of the week? Which group ate the most well-balanced meals—boys or girls?

Group Planning

A closure activity for this project is to have small groups plan a nutritious meal. They can cut out pictures from magazines and glue them to a paper plate. Or make a mobile: Attach magazine pictures or drawings of food to a coat hanger.

34

Daily Writing Activities *(cont.)*

A Week of Writing

Each day provide students with a different writing prompt and allow them five minutes to illustrate and ten minutes to write on the topic. A timer works well to remind students when their time limit is up. Writings can be kept in a spiral notebook or on large index cards. Ideas can be shared on a daily or weekly basis, or display all writing booklets at a special center. Some sample topics are listed below (for variety, list two or three choices and have students choose one to write on).

1. Write a fruit alphabet. A is for apple, B is for banana, etc	8. Write a list of five things you might hear people say in an apple orchard.
2. Write ten words that begin with or contain the same "a" sound as apple.	9. Use the following words in a creative story: runaway, clever, apple, shiny, red, farmer.
3. Name five apple products. Tell which one is your favorite and why.	10. Make an apple menu of meals for a day. Each meal should contain a different apple dish.
4. Make a chart of fruits that contain one seed and fruits that contain many seeds.	11. Draw a wanted poster for an apple. Be sure to describe its appearance and taste.
5. In your best handwriting, copy a recipe for applesauce cookies or cake.	12. Write a list of five words that describe apples. Use the words in a poem about apples.
6. In your own words explain how to bob for apples.	13. List five questions you have about apples. Tell how you would find answers to the questions.
7. Write a story about a lopsided apple. Be sure to explain how it feels to be different.	14. If you could be any kind of apple, which kind would you be and why?

Research Projects

Group students in pairs or groups of three or four. Assign a different project to each group or let them choose from a list. Some sample projects follow.

- Conduct a class survey to find out how many students like apples or give them a choice of five apple products from which to choose. Graph the results.

- Draw a tree. Label bark, root, leaf, branch, and trunk.

- Tell how insects help pollinate plants.

- Define each word. Use each one in a sentence: seed, germinate, embryo.

- Make a chart that compares two different fruits. List ways in which they are alike and ways in which they are different (color, size, number of seeds, etc.)

- Research what vitamins and minerals are contained in apples. Tell how they help your body grow.

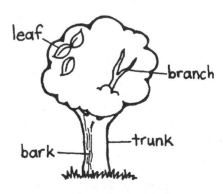

Name:	Date:

Journal Worksheet

Write the names of the foods you ate for dinner in the proper sections of the food graph. Then answer the questions below.

Food Graph

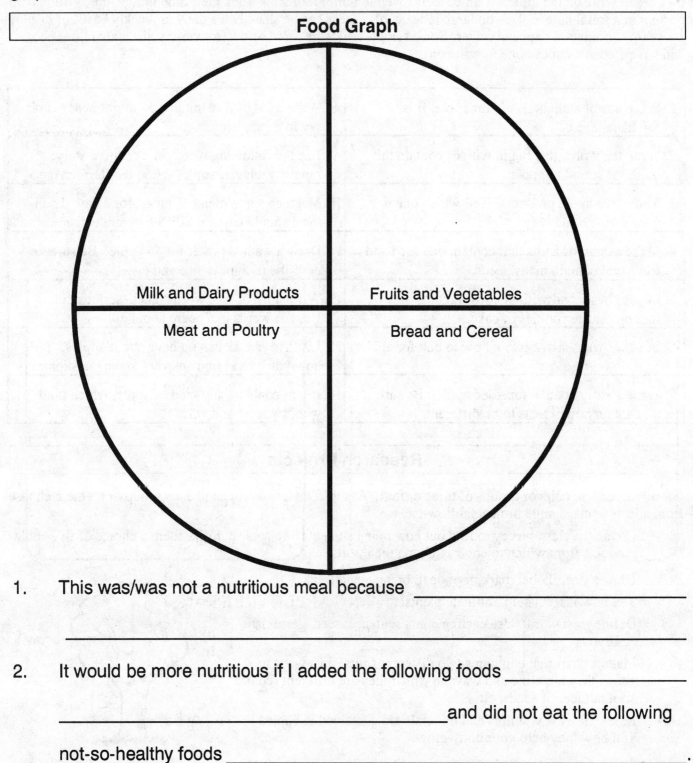

Milk and Dairy Products

Fruits and Vegetables

Meat and Poultry

Bread and Cereal

1. This was/was not a nutritious meal because _____

    _____

2. It would be more nutritious if I added the following foods _____

    _____and did not eat the following

    not-so-healthy foods _____.

Apple Word Banks

This resource page is a handy reference for various writing activities such as reports, creative writing, rhymes and poems, social studies lessons, and science experiments. In addition, these words can be used as spelling word lists and can serve as a springboard for brainstorming.

APPLE TERMS

core	flesh	potassium	round	green
seeds	pectin	skin	oval	yellow
pome	Vitamin A	sweet	preserve	hard
fruit	Vitamin C	tart	red	soft

DESCRIPTIVE WORDS

red	round	sweet	fleshy	solid	golden	ripe
yellow	oval	tart	bright	juicy	hard	rotten
green	delicious	crunchy	shiny	firm	soft	crisp

COMMON VARIETIES

*Jonathan
*Rome Beauty
*McIntosh
*Golden Delicious
Winesap
Granny Smith
*Red Delicious

*Five Most Popular in U.S.

APPLE PRODUCTS

pie
tarts
cider
applesauce
apple butter
jelly
juice
vinegar
dumplings
cake
fritters
cobbler

GROWING APPLE TREES

dormant	budding	bees	pistil
pruned	bloom	blossom	fruit
seedlings	fertilizer	petals	pesticides
grafting	pollinate	stamen	harvested

Name:	Date:

Apple Wordsearch

Hidden in this apple you will find the names of seven different kinds of apples. Circle each one. They may be forwards, backwards, or diagonal.

WORD LIST
Delicious
Pippin
Rome Beauty
Jonathan
Granny Smith
Winesap
McIntosh

```
S D F W H J K L A Q W E R T Y U
W E R T I U I O P Z X C V B N M
P T Y U F N P M C I N T O S H A
I N B V C X E Q A Z W S X E D C
P P O K M N J S U H B V G Y T F
P T G B J H Y U A M I K O L P Q
I D S E S O A E Q P R D E S W Q
N R U E Z W N V Y B U N I M O L
A R O M E B E A U T Y V G Y B H
U N I I M K O L T L K J H G F D
S A C O I U Y T R H W Q F T Y G
G T I V F R C D E X A W A S D R
F V L G T Y H B N J U N F M O L
P E E H G T E H G Y V F T F A S
D E D C H T I M S Y N N A R G W
K N Y H G T F D E C V G B N H Y
U J M A S D F G F D E S W D E F
```

38   © 1990 Teacher Created Materials, Inc.

Apple Wheel

This versatile wheel can be used for vocabulary development, creative writing, sight words, or spelling words, for example. To make an Apple Wheel, color and cut out the apple shape on this page. Then follow the directions on page 40.

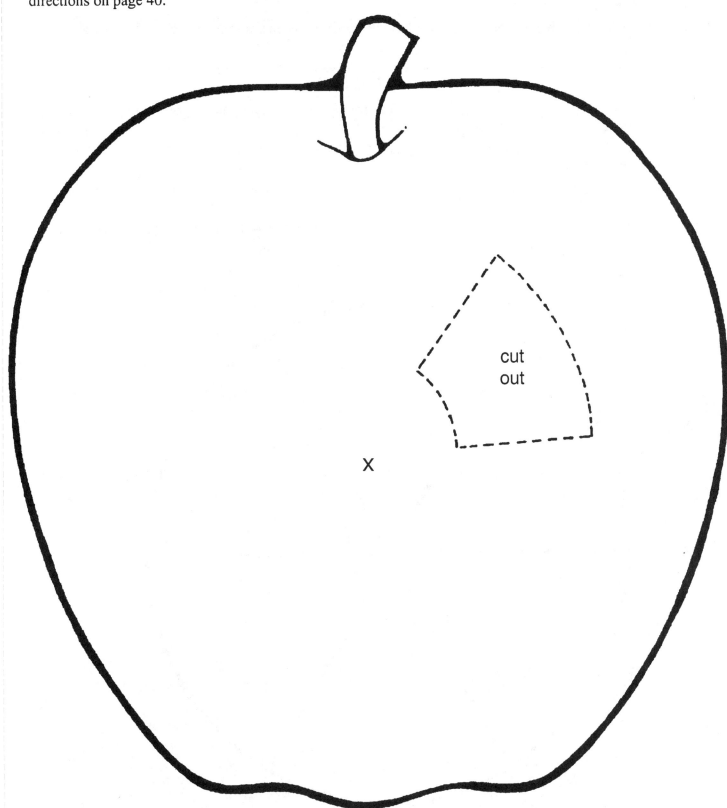

cut
out

x

     # 266 Thematic Unit — Apples

Apple Wheel *(cont.)*

Directions:

- Cut out the wheel below.
- Attach the wheel behind the apple (page 39) with a paper fastener through the center.
- Rotate the wheel and write in each space.

Suggested Uses:

- Write an adjective to describe apples in each space. Have students write a story, poem or song using as many of the words as possible.
- Write a phrase in each space, e.g. crunchy like potato chips, shiny red, etc. Students are to write each phrase in a complete sentence.
- Write a vocabulary word in each space (see page 37 for sample lists). Tell students to define each word.
- Have students write one sentence of a simple story in each space; turn the wheel to read the story.
- Make several Apple Wheels. Color each apple a different color and put a different activity on each.

Apple Writings

Begin a creative writing lesson by comparing apple products. Divide the class into five groups. Provide each group with a different food such as applesauce, apple juice, or apples of various varieties. Have them observe their food item and make a list of words that describe how that food looks, feels, smells, tastes, and sounds when being eaten. Then compile each group's words on a **Sense Matrix** (see page 42). Use this matrix as a Word Bank for creative writing projects. Some suggestions are given below.

Apple Poems

Write the word "apple" downward (or use the name of an apple such as "Winesap"). For each letter, write words or a phrase describing apples; each word or phrase should begin with, end with, or contain the letter.

> he**A**lthful
> a**P**petizing
> **P**retty and
> **L**uscious
> to **E**at.

Apple Expressions

Conduct a whole group discussion about the real meanings of these apple expressions. Then, pair the students and have them illustrate one expression. Share the pictures with the class.

She's the *apple of his eye.*

An *apple a day* keeps the doctor away.

One *rotten apple* spoils the bunch.

He has a very large *Adam's apple.*

Jeff sure knows how to *polish the apple!*

Apple Chain Story

Divide the students into teams of two or three; each team will create a story, one frame at a time. To start, one child chooses a title. The next child provides the first sentence, and so on. Each sentence is written and illustrated on a different frame (index cards work well or use the apple stationery on page 76). When completed, punch holes on opposite sides of the frames and connect them with string or yarn. Hang on the walls.

Sense Matrix for Apple Writings

(To be used with pages 6 and 41).

Sounds					
Tastes					
Feels					
Smells					
Looks					
Apple Products					

42

Name:	Date:

Same Shapes

Color the shapes.

Color Key

◯ red

☐ green

▭ blue

△ yellow

Color the shapes below that are the same as the first one in each row. Use the Color Key.

Name:	Date:

An Apple Lunch

For lunch today your mom packed all apple foods. Read the menu and answer the questions.

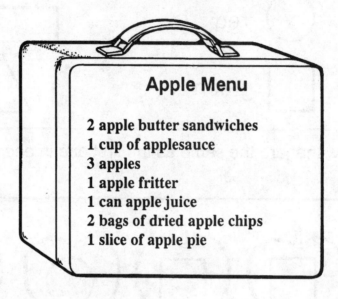

Apple Menu

2 apple butter sandwiches
1 cup of applesauce
3 apples
1 apple fritter
1 can apple juice
2 bags of dried apple chips
1 slice of apple pie

1. How many things are in your lunch altogether? _____

2. You gave a friend one apple. How many foods are left? _____

3. Then you gave the apple pie to your teacher and 1 apple butter sandwich to your best friend. Now how many foods are left? _____

4. Make a list of the foods that are left in your lunch bag.

    _____   _____

    _____   _____

    _____   _____

    _____   _____

    Put a star (*) next to your favorite food on the list.

44

Name:	Date:

Apple Word Problems

Teacher: These problems may be cut out and glued to index cards or to an apple for the *Apple Time* Bulletin Board. Students can solve problems with a partner.

1. Which apple is cut in fourths?

a   b   c

2. 12 's

José ate 4.

How many left?

3. 6 's
3 's   4 's

How many altogether?

4. 10 's on a 🌳

3 's fell.

How many 's left on the 🌳?

5. 3 🌳's

3 's on each 🌳

How many altogether?

6. Which apple is cut in half?

a   b   c

7. 7 's

4 more 's.

How many altogether?

8. 15 's

Only 5 's have 🐛's.

How many 's do not have 🐛's?

Name: | Date:

Mystery Dot-to-Dot

Find out how the flower is getting pollen. Count by twos and connect the dots.
Color the picture.

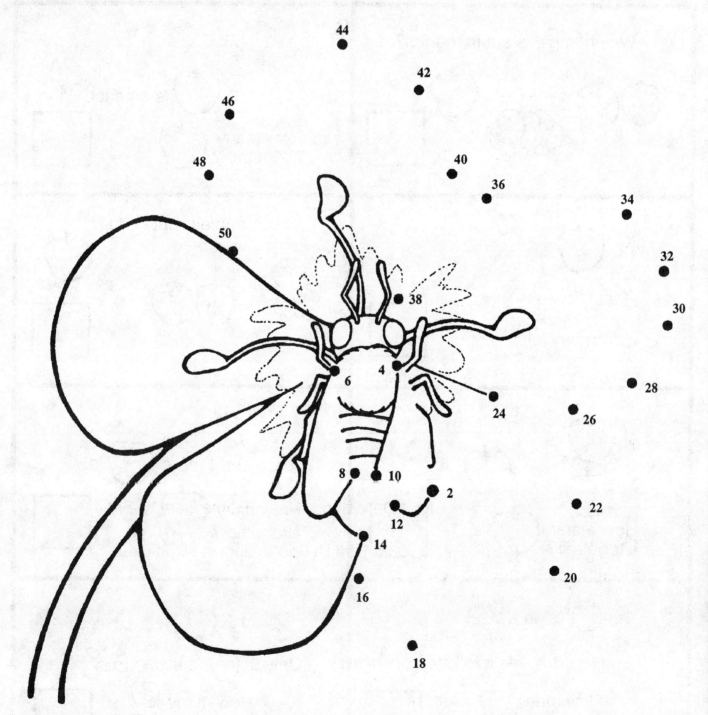

Trace the word.

The flower is getting pollen from a honeybee

     46

Name:	Date:

Cooking with Apples

Mom used apples to make cookies, cider, and applesauce. Here is a picture graph of the apples she used. Read the graph. Circle the answers.

1. This graph shows how many
    a. apples Mom likes
    b. the best kind of apples
    c. apples Mom used in cooking

2. The number of Pippin apples used was
    a. nine   b. twelve   c. eight

3. Mom used the fewest
    a. Pippin   b. Red Delicious   c. Rome Beauty

4. Mom used the most
    a. Pippin   b. Red Delicious   c. Rome Beauty

5. The number of Rome Beauty and Red Delicious apples Mom used altogether was
    a. 16   b. 18   c. 19

6. From the graph you can tell
    a. there are only three kinds of apples.
    b. Mom used Red Delicious apples the most.
    c. Mom likes to cook.

Name:	Date:

Apples Are Good for You

Find out why apples are so good for you. Cut and paste the words below. Read the sentence.

1. Apples have very little

2. A small apple has about 80

3. Apples have [   ] which helps our bodies stay healthy.

4. Apples also have [   ] which keeps our bones strong.

5. The [   ] in apples helps to digest food.

6. Apples have very little [   ], or salt.

calories.	pectin	Vitamin A
(2)	(5)	(3)
sodium	Vitamin C	fat.
(6)	(4)	(1)

Name:	Date:

The Food Groups

Our bodies need different kinds of foods to grow and stay healthy. To help us know what to eat, food is divided into five groups. Circle and color the foods that belong in each group. Cross out the one that doesn't belong.

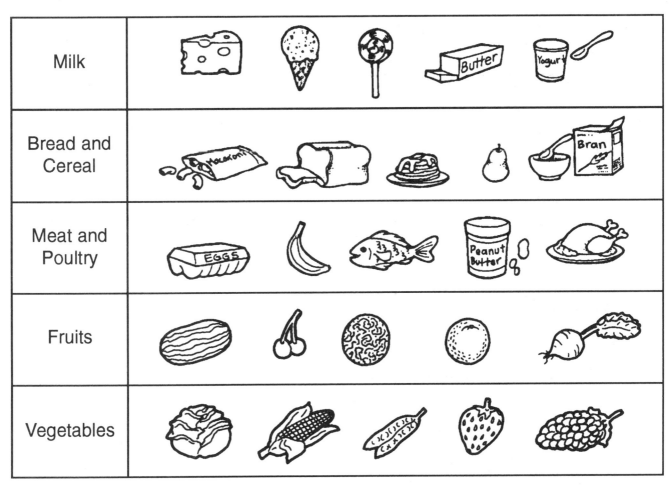

Milk	
Bread and Cereal	
Meat and Poultry	
Fruits	
Vegetables	

Remember to eat the right number of servings from each food group every day. Unscramble the words to find out how much you need from each group.

1. Eat (wot) _ _ _ or three servings of milk and milk products.

2. You need (sxi) _ _ _ to eleven servings of bread and cereal.

3. You should eat (tow) _ _ _ or three servings of meat and poultry.

4. Eat (rethe) _ _ _ _ _ or four servings of fruits.

5. You should eat (rethe) _ _ _ _ _ to five servings of vegetables.

Name:	Date:

Seasons of a Tree

Match the picture to the season. Write the sentences in order on the lines below.

3.
The apples are ready to be picked.

spring

4.
The tree can rest—no more apples.

summer

2.
The apples grow bigger every day.

fall

1.
The apple blossoms begin to grow.

winter

1. _____

2. _____

3. _____

4. _____

Name:	Date:

Parts Of An Apple Flower

Work with a partner. Label the parts of this apple flower. Use words from the Word Bank below.

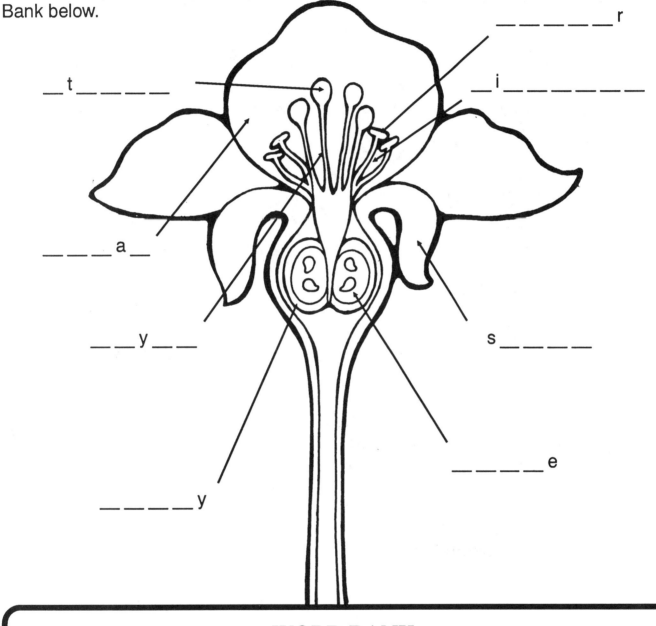

_ _ _ _ _ _ r

_ t _ _ _ _ _

_ _ i _ _ _ _ _ _

_ _ _ _ a _

_ _ y _ _

s _ _ _ _ _

_ _ _ _ e

_ _ _ _ _ y

WORD BANK

filament	stigma	style	ovule
anther	ovary	sepal	petal

Teacher: You may wish to enlarge this for a wall chart to which students can refer if the activity is too difficult for your group.

Name:	Date:

Seeds

There are many kinds of seeds. Color the seeds in each of the foods below.

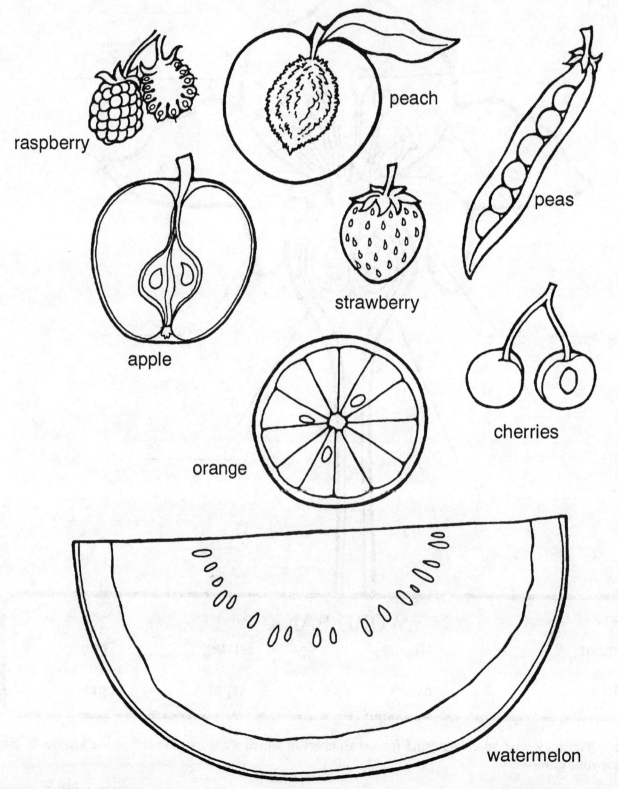

raspberry

peach

peas

apple

strawberry

cherries

orange

watermelon

"A Is for Apple" Gameboard

Color, cut out and glue the gameboard to the inside of a file folder. Then cut out the directions (page 54) and glue to the front of the file folder. Cut apart the task cards (page 54). Store in an envelope attached to the back of the file folder. Laminate the file folder and task cards for durability.

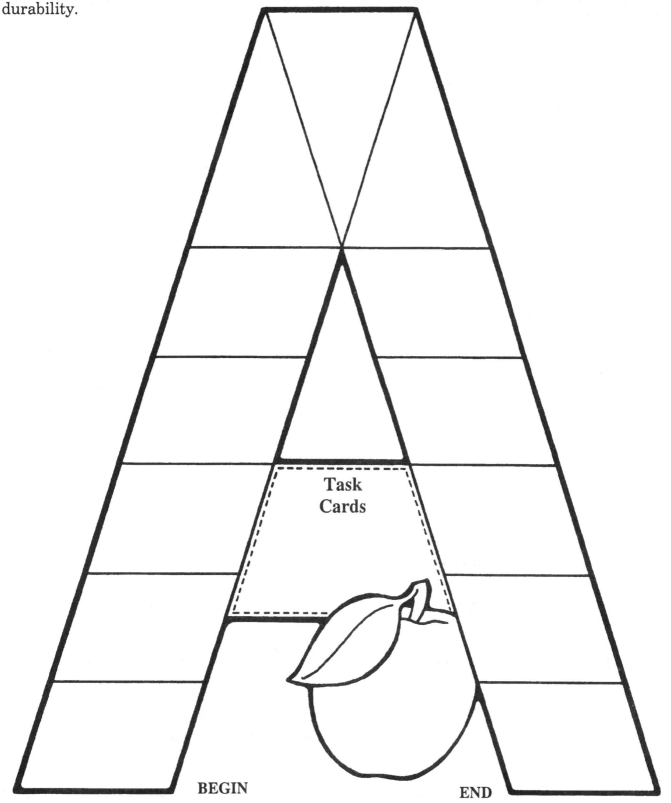

Task Cards

BEGIN

END

"A Is for Apple" Gameboard (cont.)

Directions:

This game is for two or three players. Or, two teams of two players each may play. Teams act as one player but they can determine an answer together. Each player will need a marker. Use a die or a spinner that has only ones and twos on it.

1. Place the Task Cards in a pile on the gameboard.

2. Take a task card and answer the question.

3. If you answer correctly, roll the die and move that many spaces.

4. If you answer incorrectly, stay on the same space.

5. The first player or team to reach the **END** wins.

Task Cards

Use these or make your own. Have books available so students may research answers they do not know. To make this game self-correcting, number each card. Write the answer next to the corresponding number on a separate sheet of paper. (See Answer Key, page 80.)

Name one animal that lives in a tree. **1.**	What do tree roots get from the soil? **6.**	Name one way that seeds are moved. **11.**	What is one thing a seed needs in order to grow? **16.**	What are two foods made from apples? **21.**
What insect helps pollinate apple trees? **2.**	Why does a tree need bark? **7.**	Name two things that come from trees. **12.**	Why do flowers make pollen? **17.**	Who was Johnny Appleseed? **22.**
Name a fruit that has only one seed. **3.**	How does a tree take in air? **8.**	Name two fruits that grow on trees. **13.**	Which state grows the most apples? **18.**	Name one insect that lives on a tree. **23.**
Name a fruit that has many seeds. **4.**	The color ____ helps leaves make food. **9.**	Name one part of a flower. **14.**	Tell one reason why apples are good for you. **19.**	In what season do trees grow blossoms? **24.**
Name one kind of apple. **5.**	In what season do trees lose their leaves? **10.**	What is the tiny plant inside a seed called? **15.**	Name two fruits that are made into jam or jelly. **20.**	What is your favorite apple dish? **25.**

54

Name:	Date:

Hidden Picture

Color each space **YELLOW** that has the name of a fruit.

Color each space **RED** that has the name of a vegetable.

Color the empty space **GREEN.**

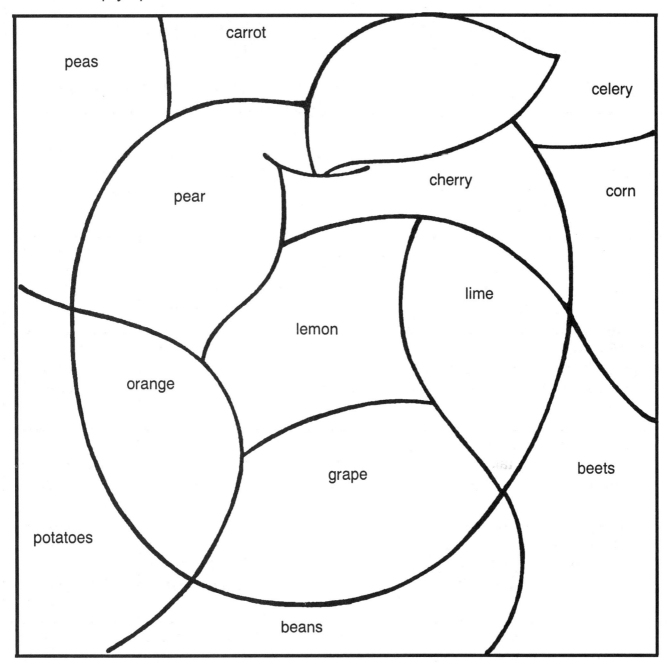

Trace the letters.

This apple is a Golden Delicious.

Name:	Date:

Apple Customs

Long, long ago in England games were played with apples at Halloween time.

1. On Snap Apple Night boys tried to bite an apple that twirled from the end of a stick.

2. In Bobbing for Apples, apples floated in a pan of water. If a boy caught an apple with his teeth, it meant his girlfriend loved him.

3. Girls Peeled an Apple. Then they tossed the peel over their shoulder to see if it would form the first letter of their true love's name.

Now see if you can match the picture to the name of the game. Color the picture of the game you like best.

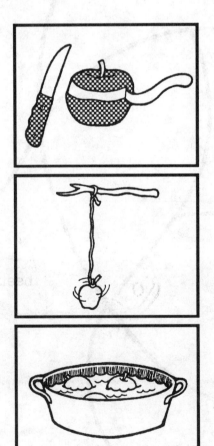

Snap Apple Night

Bobbing for Apples

Peel an Apple

Note: For more information on Halloween customs read *Halloween* by Joyce K. Kessel.

56

| Name: | Date: |

An Orchard Map

Look at the map of the orchard. Follow the directions below.

1. Draw a **green** path from the truck to the barn.

2. Draw a **yellow** path from the apple picker to the truck.

3. Draw a **blue** path from the beehive to all the trees.

4. Draw **red** apples on the trees.

Name:	Date:

From Tree to Market

Color and cut apart the pictures. Paste them in order in the frame below.

1.	**2.**	**3.**	**4.**

Tell a story. Write a sentence about each picture in order.

1. _____

_____

_____

2. _____

_____

_____

3. _____

_____

_____

4. _____

_____

_____

Apple Orchards

In the spring, farmers put hives of honeybees in the apple orchards. They want to make sure that the bees bring pollen to the apple flowers. Make a picture of an apple orchard. Cut apart the puzzle pieces below and glue them into the frame. Color the picture.

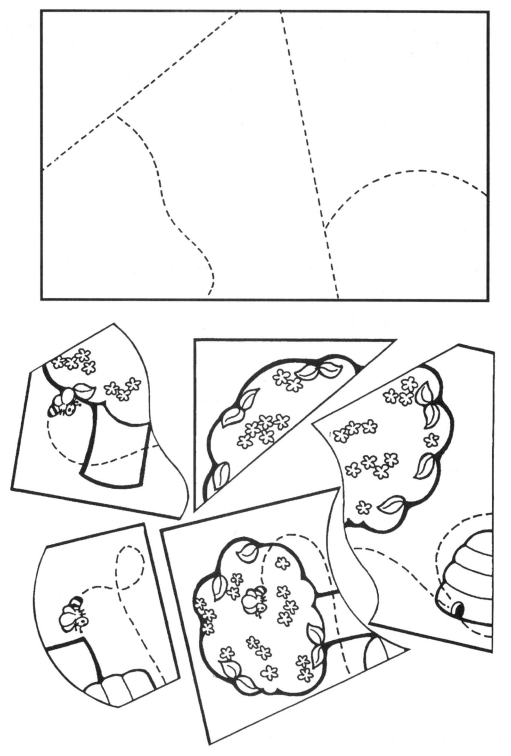

Name:	Date:

You Can Draw It!

Copy the picture one square at a time onto the bottom grid. Color your picture.

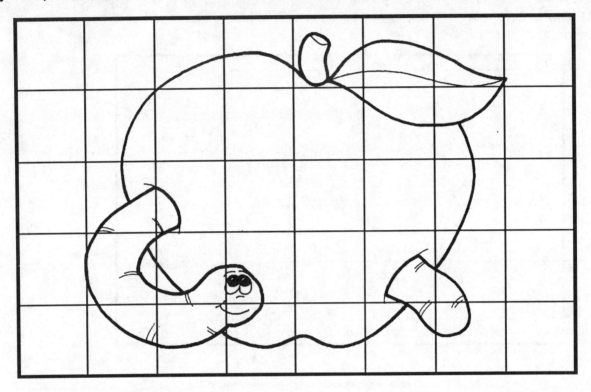

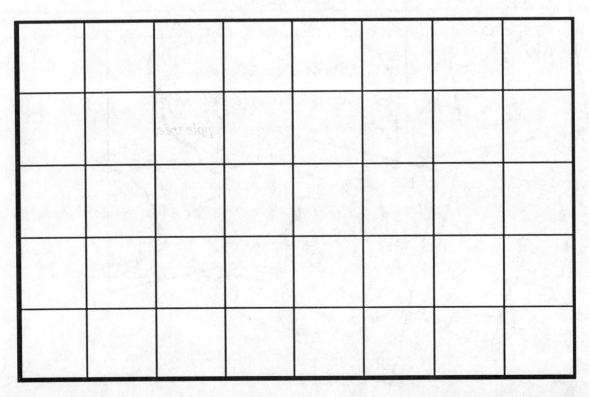

Creative Movement

Bobbing for Apples

You don't have to wait for Halloween to bob for apples. And this version will not get you wet! Just fill a container with foam packing peanuts and add some apples. To play, blindfold the child. Instruct him to keep his arms behind his back as he bobs for apples.

A Growing Experience

Have the students pretend they are seeds by curling up their bodies. As you tell them a story about how a seed grows, direct students to move accordingly. For example, as the seed reaches upward toward the ground, the students can stretch upward as they try to break through the earth. As the seed sprouts, have the students move their arms expansively. Play soft music in the background to enhance the mood.

Spring, Summer, Fall, Winter

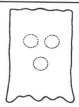

Make tree masks for the seasons (see pages 62 and 63 for patterns). Have students explain what it feels like to be a tree in autumn when all its apples are being picked. Or tell how the blossoms make it feel in the spring. Move like trees in a wind storm, a gentle rain, or a snowfall. These masks can also be used to reenact scenes from *The Giving Tree*.

Round the Apple Tree

Play a singing circle game to the tune of "Here We Go Round the Mulberry Bush." Children skip in a circle, holding hands, while singing the first verse.

> **Verse 1:** *Here we go round the apple tree,*
>
> *The apple tree, the apple tree.*
>
> *Here we go round the apple tree,*
>
> *So early in the morning.*

On subsequent verses children stop circling and create motions to illustrate the words.

> **Verse 2:** *This is the way we plant the seeds.*
>
> **Verse 3:** *This is the way the little seed sprouts.*
>
> **Verse 4:** *This is the way it grows to a tree.*
>
> **Verse 5:** *This is the way the flowers blossom.*
>
> **Verse 6:** *This is the way the apples grow.*
>
> **Verse 7:** *This is the way the apples are picked.*
>
> Repeat verse 1.

Tree Mask

Make apple trees for each season. Add leaves for summer, apples for autumn, bare branches for winter, and blossoms for spring (patterns are on page 64). Duplicate tree pattern onto brown construction paper. Cut out eyes and mouth holes. Attach a craft stick to the bottom of the mask. Or punch holes on either side of the mask and attach yarn or string. Use for activities described on page 61.

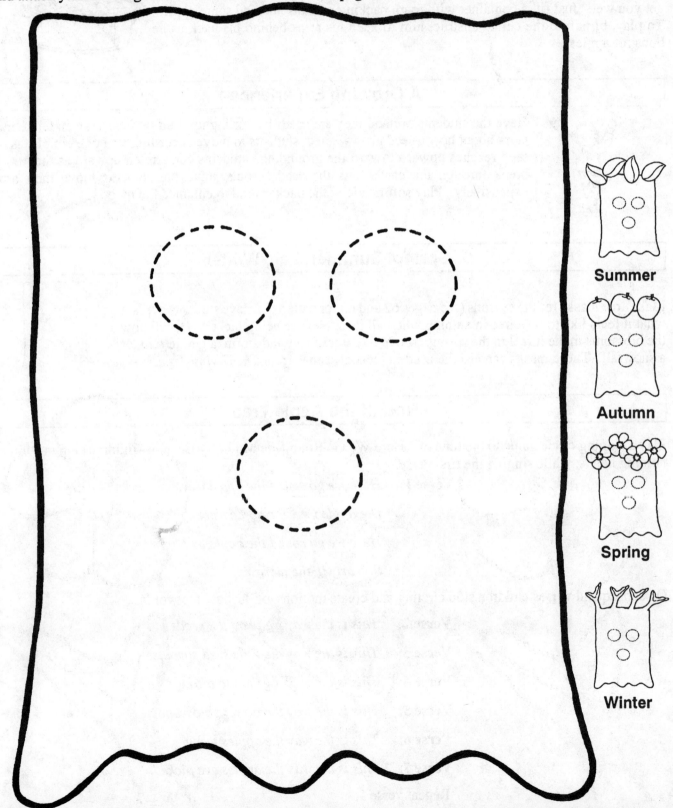

Summer

Autumn

Spring

Winter

Tree Mask *(cont.)*

Make as many of these patterns as you will need. Duplicate onto appropriately colored construction paper. Glue or staple to the top of the tree pattern (page 63).

Summer Leaves

Fall Apples

Spring Blossoms

Winter Bare Branches

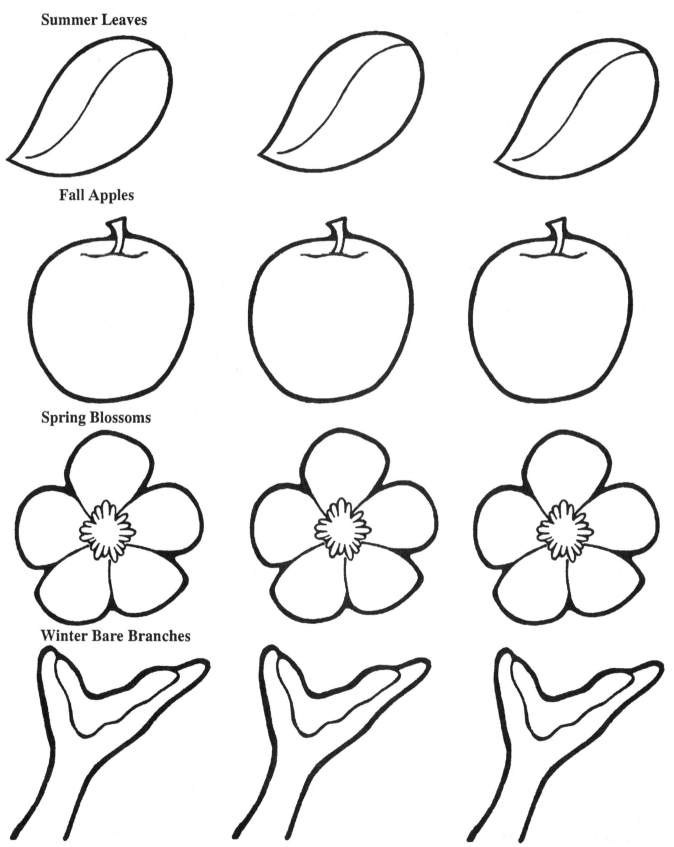

Good Enough to Eat!

Have your class make one, two, or all three of these apple treats. They're quick and easy, and yummy, too!

An Apple Smile

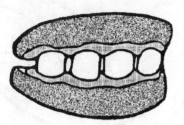

Core and slice an apple. Spread peanut butter on one side of each apple slice. Place four tiny marshmallows on top of the peanut butter of one slice. Top with another apple slice, peanut butter side down. Gently squeeze together. Enjoy!

Homemade Applesauce

- Peel, core, and slice the apples.
- Place apple slices and water in a saucepan.
- Cover and cook until tender (approximately 25 minutes).
- Add honey and cinnamon to taste.
- Makes 12 small servings.

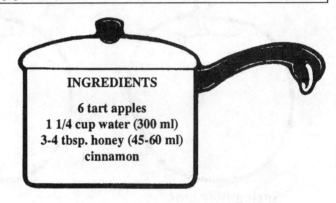

INGREDIENTS

6 tart apples
1 1/4 cup water (300 ml)
3-4 tbsp. honey (45-60 ml)
cinnamon

Apple-Cheddar Grilled Sandwich

INGREDIENTS

For each sandwich you will need:

- **two slices of bread (whole wheat or raisin bread are especially tasty!)**
- **cheddar cheese slices**
- **apples slices (thin)**
- **butter**

- Melt a pat of butter in a frying pan. (An electric fry pan works well.)
- Spread butter on one side of each slice of bread.
- Place one slice of bread, butter side down, in the pan.
- Put cheddar cheese slices on top and cover with apple slices.
- Lay second piece of bread on top, butter side up.
- Cook till cheese begins to melt.
- Turn over; cook till other side of bread is browned.

Tasty Apple Treats

Apples are delicious any way they are served: raw, cooked, or baked. Try these two recipes with your students for unusual, easy-to-make snacks.

Stuffed Apples

Ingredients: one apple per person; butter or margarine; brown sugar; raisins; dates; shredded coconut; chopped pecans or walnuts; whipped cream (optional)

Directions:

- Core the apples with an apple corer; sprinkle the inside of the apple with some brown sugar.
- Place the apples into a greased baking dish.
- Stuff the apples with the dates, raisins, coconut, and nuts. (Allow students to choose their own stuffings.)
- Pour in enough warm water to cover the bottom of the baking dish.
- Bake at 350 degrees F for 35 to 45 minutes.
- Baste the apples with juice from the dish twice during baking.
- Allow the apples to cool before eating.

Sun Dried Apples

Ingredients: small apples, one for each student

Directions:

- Core the apples with an apple corer.
- Thread string through the cored apples; tie knots.
- Hang the apples from a central string outside in the sun.
- When the apples have dried, remove the strings and eat.

Note: Apples can be hung from an oven rack at a very low temperature, 150 degrees F., to dry.

Apple Fest

An Apple Fest is a fun way to culminate your apple studies. Set up four centers in your room (complete directions are below) and invite parents, other classes, or the principal to your celebration. Serve some class-made apple refreshments for a perfect final touch.

- Students can write their own invitations using the Newsletter or Invitation form found on page 78.

- Set up four centers in the classroom. At one, display students' creative writing samples such as Wheel Books, their daily writing activities, and original poems. A second center can be designated for science activities. Students can exhibit seedlings they have grown, the From Seed to Apple flap book, and Parts of a Tree chart. The third center can be a simple art activity for participants to complete right there. Sample project ideas are apple tree prints (page 67), contour apples (page 67), or a graph drawing (page 61). Finally, prepare homemade apple butter (recipe is on page 67), and serve it on bread or crackers. Beverages could include apple juice or cider.

- For a more organized time, divide the participants into groups and cycle them from center to center. Explain the centers to the whole group. Tell them the order in which one center will move to the next. Set a time limit. At a given signal everyone moves to the next center.

- October is **National Apple Month**. If possible, conduct your apple unit and culminating Apple Fest during that month.

Apple Fest *(cont.)*

Apple Butter

Ingredients: ten apples; 1/2 cup water; sugar; 1 tsp. cinnamon

Directions:

- Peel and core the apples; slice thinly.
- Place the apple slices into a saucepan.
- Add the half cup of water.
- Cook on medium heat until the apples are soft.
- Mash the pulp with a potato masher or a fork.
- Add one half cup of sugar for every cup of pulp.
- Add one teaspoon of cinnamon.
- Cook on low until thick and dark.
- Spread on bread or crackers.

Contour Apples

Materials: drawing paper or construction paper; black marker; crayons

Directions:

- With the marking pen, draw a bold outline of an apple (or apple tree).
- Then repeat the outline starting on the inside close to the shape's edge (see illustration at right).
- Continue to redraw the outline smaller and smaller until it cannot be repeated any more.
- Now color in each contour with a different color.

Apple Tree Prints

Materials: apples cut in half; thin green and red tempera paint; light brown construction paper; black marker or crayon

Directions:

- Press cut half of apple into green paint and press onto construction paper to form leaves (see diagram at right). Let dry.
- Press a thumb into the red paint and then onto the leaves to make apples.
- Draw a trunk with marker or crayon.

67

Bulletin Board

Objectives

This interactive bulletin board can be used as part of an Apple Activity Center. It can also be adapted to use as reinforcement for math, reading, and language skills.

Materials

Colored construction paper or butcher paper; scissors; stapler; thick green craft yarn; pushpins

Construction

- Reproduce patterns (pages 69-73) onto appropriately colored construction paper and cut out.
- Assemble all pieces onto the bulletin board background; attach with staples or pushpins.
- Use the yarn to make grass and the tree top (see diagram above).
- Make as many apples as needed. Label as directed below.

Directions

- Label each apple with a different idea or activity. Students can choose one to do as a cooperative project or they can be used as "free time" activities. Some examples follow. Copy a recipe for apple pie in your best handwriting. Explain why New York City is called the "Big Apple." Find a recipe for applesauce; halve it; then double it (on paper!); convert it to metric measure.
- Write words on the apples on the tree. Label the apples in the basket with synonyms (or antonyms). Direct students to match the words on the tree with their synonyms (or antonyms, or both!).
- Make a black construction paper hole on the trunk. Make one apple for each student; label with their names. Place the names in a basket. Students then put their apple in the hole when they leave the room (to go to the restroom or library, etc.). When they return, they put their apple back in the basket.

68

Apple Time Bulletin Board *(cont.)*

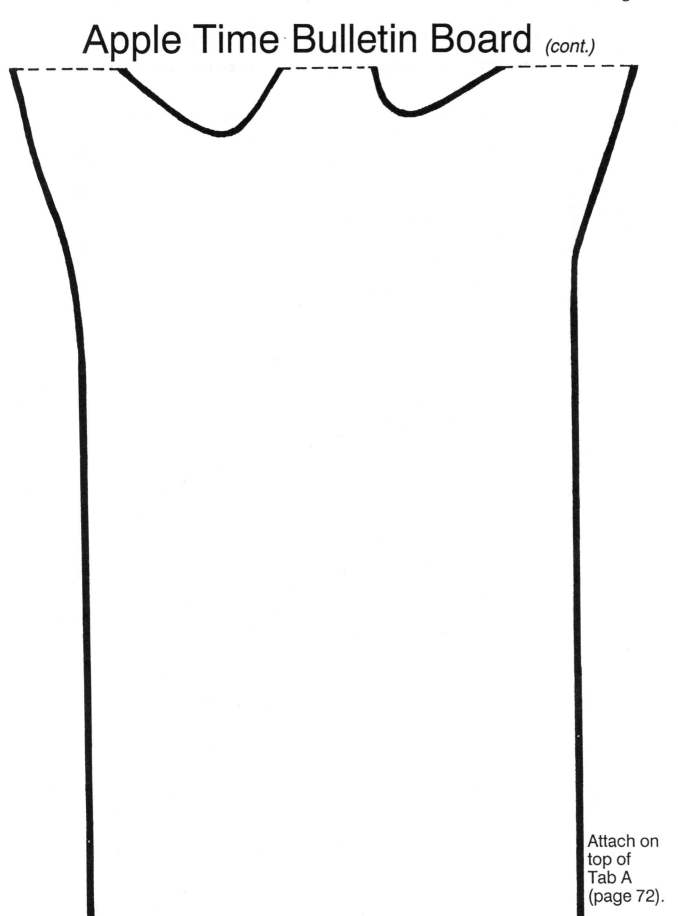

Attach on
top of
Tab A
(page 72).

Apple Time Bulletin Board *(cont.)*

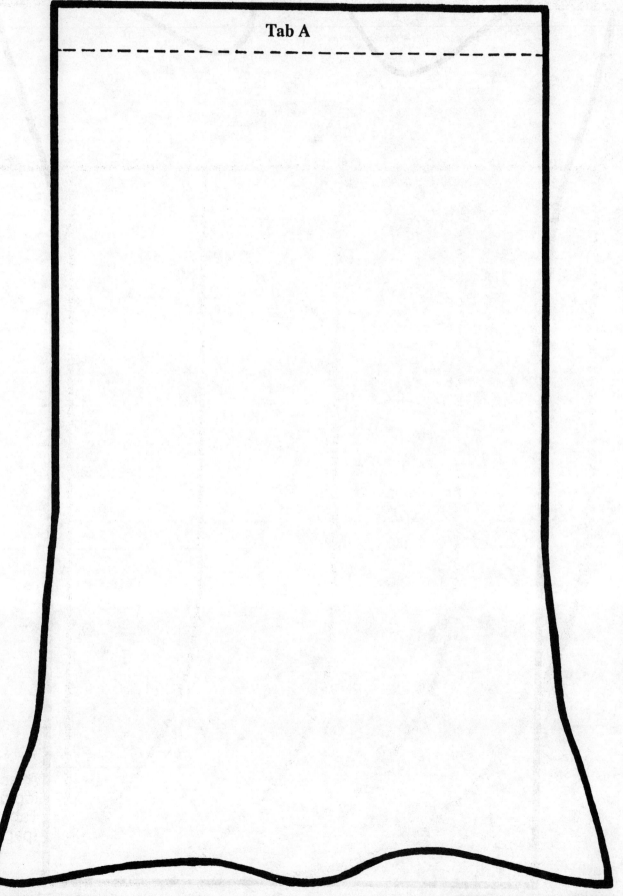

Tab A

70

Apple Time Bulletin Board *(cont.)*

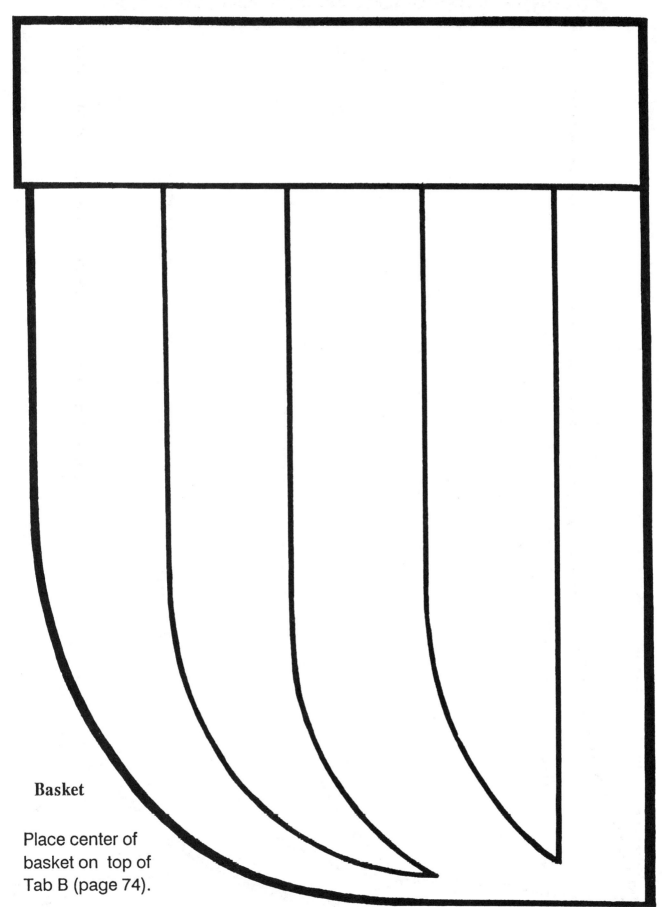

Basket

Place center of
basket on top of
Tab B (page 74).

Apple Time Bulletin Board *(cont.)*

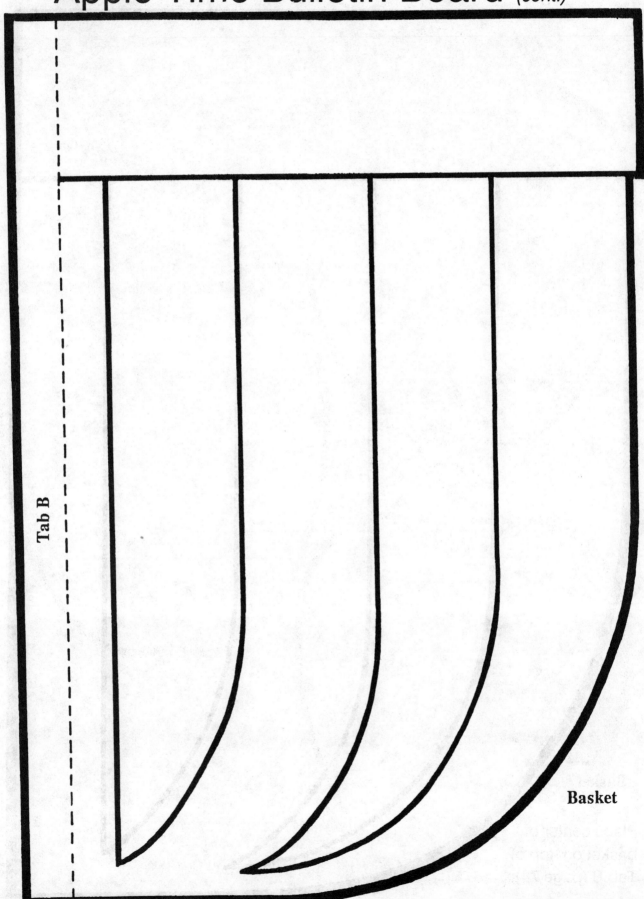

Tab B

Basket

Apple Time Bulletin Board *(cont.)*

Apples

Make as many as you need.

Calendar

month

Sunday	Monday	Tuesday	Wednesday	Thursday	Friday	Saturday

Name:	Date

Learning Center Record Keeper

Write the name of a different Learning Center project on each apple. As you complete each project, write in the day's date and color the apple.

Project:
_____
Date Completed:
_____

Project:
_____
Date Completed:
_____

Project:
_____
Date Completed:
_____

Project:
_____
Date Completed:
_____

Project:
_____
Date Completed:
_____

Project:
_____
Date Completed:
_____

Project:
_____
Date Completed:
_____

Project:
_____
Date Completed:
_____

Stationery

Awards

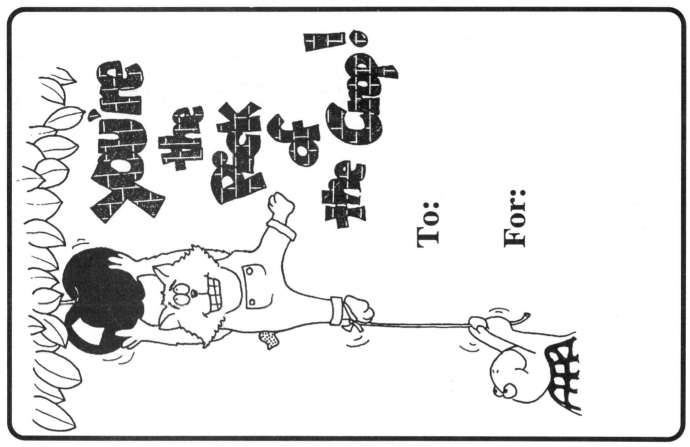

You're the Pick of the Crop

To:

For:

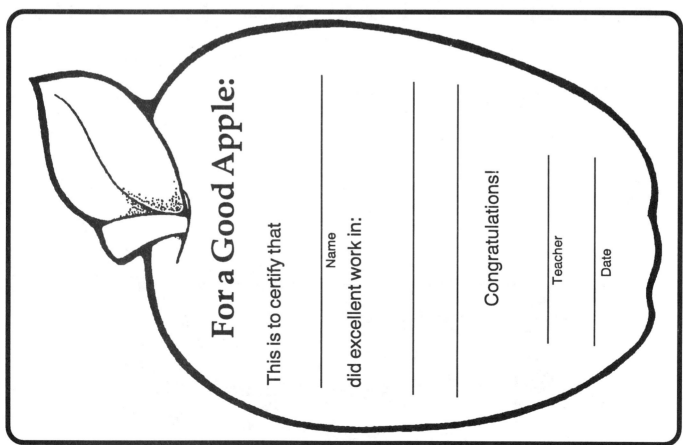

For a Good Apple:

This is to certify that

_____
Name

did excellent work in:

_____

_____

Congratulations!

_____
Teacher

_____
Date

Newsletter/Invitation

Word's Out!

Who:

What:

Where:

When:

What:

Where:

When:

Bibliography

Fiction

Aesop's Fables. Avenel Books, 1912 (or other collection)

Aliki. *The Story of Johnny Appleseed.* Prentice-Hall, 1963

Asch, Frank. *Oats and Wild Apples.* Holiday House, 1988

Cooney, Barbara. *Miss Rumphius.* Puffin Books, 1985

Dewey, Ariane. *Gib Morgan, Oilman.* Greenwillow, 1987.

Dewey, Ariane. *Pecos Bill.* Greenwillow, 1983

Elrich, Amy. *Pome & Peel.* Dial, 1990

Forest, Heather. *The Baker's Dozen: A Colonial American Tale.* Harcourt, 1988

Gelter, Jan & Kathleen Thompson. *Paul Bunyan and Babe the Blue Ox.* Raintree, 1985

Jensen, Patsy. *Johnny Appleseed Goes a` Planting.* Troll Associates, 1994.

Keats, Ezra Jack. *John Henry: An American Legend.* Pantheon, 1965

Kellog, Steven. *Johnny Appleseed.* Morrow, 1988

Kellog, Steven. *Paul Bunyan.* Morrow, 1984

Kellog, Steven. *Pecos Bill.* Morrow, 1986

Krauss, Ruth. *The Carrot Seed. Scholastic, 1985*

Lobel, Arnold. *Fables.* Harper & Row, 1980

Parish, Peggy. *Teach Us, Amelia Bedelia.* Scholastic, 1987

Prelutsky, Jack. Random *House Book of Poetry for Children.* Random House, 1983

Scheer, Julian. *Rain Makes Applesauce.* Holiday House, 1964

Seuss, Dr. *To Think That I Saw It On Mulberry Street*, Random House, 1937, 1989.

Silverstein, Shel. *The Giving Tree.* Harper and Row, 1964

Udry, Janet. *A Tree is Nice.* Harper Junior Books, 1956

Nonfiction

Gibbons, Gail. *The Seasons of Arnold's Apple Tree.* HBJ, 1984

Ingoglia, Gina. *Look Inside a Tree.* Grosset & Dunlap, 1989

Jennings, Terry. *The Young Scientist Investigates Food.* Children's Press, 1984

Jennings, Terry. *The Young Scientist Investigates Seeds and Seedlings.* Children's Press, 1981

Johnson, Hannah Lyons. *From Apple Seed to Applesauce.* Lothrop, Lee and Shepard Company, 1987

Kessel, Joyce K. *Halloween.* Carolrhoda, 1980

Selsam, Millicent E. *The Apple and Other Fruits.* Morrow, 1973

Trees. Usborne First Nature Books, EDC Publishing, 1980

Watts, Barrie. *Apple Tree.* Silver Burdett, 1987.

Teacher Created Materials

104 *Big and Easy Health*

212 *Food and Nutrition*

229 *Problem-Solving Science Investigations*

Answer Key

p. 12

Color sentences 1,2,4,6

p. 14

Across:	Down:
2. apple	1. tales
5. September	2. autumn
6. Ohio	3. Chapman
7. bear	4. orchards

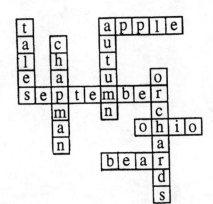

p. 23

1. loved	4. sad
2. happy	5. tired
3. alone	6. happy

p. 26

First, the boy plays...

Second, the boy gathers...

Third, the boy uses...

Fourth, the boy cuts...

Fifth, the boy sits...

p. 27

Tree stump-I have
  nothing left...

Old Man-I want a boat...

Tree-Take my apples...

Young Man-I want to buy...

Very Old Man-I don't need...

p. 38

Apple Wordsearch

```
S D F W H J K L A Q W E R T Y U
W E R T I U I O P Z X C V B N M
P T Y U F N P M C I N T O S H A
I N B V C X E Q A Z W S X E D C
P P O K M N J S U H B V G Y T F
P T G B U H Y U A M I K O L P Q
I D S E S O A E Q P R D E S W Q
N R U E Z W N V Y B U N I M O L
A R O M E B E A U T Y V G Y B H
U N T I M K O L T L K J H G F D
S A C O I U Y T R H W Q F T Y G
G T I V F R C D E X A W A S D R
F V L G T Y H B N J U N F M O L
P E E H G T E H G Y V F T F A S
D E O C H T I M S Y N N A R G W
K N Y H G T F D E C V G B N H Y
U J M A S D F G F D E S W D E F
```

p. 44

1. 11
2. 10
3. 8
4. 1 apple butter sandwich,
   1 cup applesauce, 2 apples,
   1 apple fritter, 1 can apple
   juice, 2 bags dried apple chips

p. 45

1. b		5. 9
2. 8		6. b
3. 13		7. 11
4. 7		8. 10

p. 47

1. c		4. b
2. a		5. c
3. c		6. b

p. 48

1. fat		4. Vitamin C
2. calories		5. pectin
3. Vitamin A		6. sodium

p. 49

1. two	3. two	5. three
2. six	4. three	

p. 51

Parts of an Apple Flower

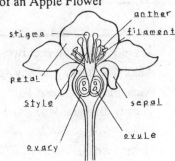

p. 54

1. squirrel, bird, monkey, etc.
2. bee
3. peach, plum, avocado, etc.
4. apple, orange, grape, berries, etc.
5. McIntosh, Delicious, Pippin, Rome Beauty, Jonathan, Granny Smith, Winesap, etc.
6. water and minerals
7. to protect it from insects, disease, and drying out
8. through tiny holes on the underside of their leaves
9. green
10. autumn, fall
11. birds, wind, animals, water, etc.
12. fruit, wood, paper, nuts, etc.
13. pear, apple, banana, peach, plum, orange, lemon, lime, etc.
14. filament, stigma, style, ovule, anther, carpel, ovary, sepal, petal, etc.
15. embryo plant
16. water, sunlight, oxygen from the air
17. so seeds can be formed
18. Washington
19. low fat, Vitamin A & C, low sodium, few calories, pectin for digestion
20. berries, apples, oranges, peaches, pears, plums, etc.
21. juice, pie, cobbler, jam or jelly, cider, vinegar, applesauce, etc.
22. John Chapman who started orchards for the pioneers
23. caterpillars, moths, beetles, termites, etc.
24. spring
25. Answers will vary.